GREAT
MOMENTS
IN
BASEBALL
HISTORY

GREAT MOMENTS IN BASEBALL HISTORY

MATT CHRISTOPHER®

LITTLE, BROWN AND COMPANY

New York ↬ Boston

To my son, Marty

Little, Brown and Company

Hachette Book Group USA
237 Park Avenue, New York, NY 10020
Visit our Web site at www.lb-kids.com

www.mattchristopher.com

First Edition

Matt Christopher® is a registered trademark
of Matt Christopher Royalties, Inc.

Library of Congress Cataloging-in-Publication Data

Christopher, Matt.
     Great moments in baseball history / by Matt Christopher. — 1st ed.
         p. cm.
     Summary: Describes nine memorable moments from baseball's past, featuring Bill Wambsganss, Babe Ruth, Joe Nuxhall, Willie Mays, Ted Williams, Reggie Jackson, Dave Dravecky, Kirk Gibson, and Jim Abbott.
     ISBN 978-0-316-14130-7
     1. Baseball — United States — History — Juvenile literature.
2. Baseball players — United States — Biography — Juvenile literature.
[1. Baseball — History. 2. Baseball players] I. Title.
GV863.A1C44 1996
796.357'0973 — dc20   95-36956

20 19 18 17 16 15 14 13 12 11

COM-MO

Printed in the United States of America

CONTENTS

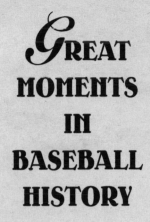

GREAT MOMENTS IN BASEBALL HISTORY

BILL WAMBSGANSS
The Man Who Was Ready

One play made all the difference.

If not for one spectacular play he made in the 1920 World Series, second baseman Bill Wambsganss would be remembered only for his hard-to-pronounce last name. But because Bill Wambsganss was ready, because he was constantly thinking ahead and preparing himself for every possible situation on the field, his name is known to baseball fans as more than just a confusing collection of letters.

Just by being ready, Bill Wambsganss set a perfect example for young ballplayers. He made a play so special that it is still remembered more than seventy-five years after it happened.

Bill Wambsganss was born in Cleveland in 1894. His parents were German, and their last name is a combination of two old German words that mean "overcoat."

3

The name looks harder to pronounce than it really is. When most people read it, they try to pronounce the *m*, the *b*, the *s*, and the *g* all at the same time. Somewhere in the middle, they trip over their tongues, and the name comes out as sounding like "WAM-bus-gans."

But here's the trick: The *b* is silent, as in *lamb,* so the correct pronunciation is "WAMZ-gans." But for most of Wambsganss's career, baseball games were not broadcast on the radio, so very few people knew the *b* was silent. All they saw was an assortment of letters in the box score printed in the newspaper. And because the name was so long, it was often abbreviated as "Wm'b'gns," which only added to the confusion.

Most of Wambsganss's friends and teammates avoided the problem altogether. They called him plain old Bill, or Wamby for short. They didn't care how his last name was pronounced. All they knew was that he was a pretty good ballplayer, and that was all that mattered.

Wambsganss started playing in the big leagues in 1914 with Cleveland. At the time, the Cleveland team was called the Naps after their star second baseman Napoleon Lajoie (his name looks difficult to pronounce, too: it's LA-zho-way). Lajoie was one of the greatest players in baseball, but by the time Bill Wambsganss joined the team, he was getting ready to retire. After backing up Lajoie for a season, Wambsganss became Cleveland's starting second baseman in 1915.

Although Wambsganss was no Napoleon Lajoie, he proved himself to be a solid all-around player. He hit about .260 or .270, stole up to 18 bases a season, and was one of the best fielding second basemen in the league. He wasn't flashy, but he was steady. He made the plays everyone expected him to make.

After Lajoie retired, the team's name changed to the Indians. In 1920, for the first time ever, they won the American League pennant, edging out Chicago, New York, and St. Louis in a close race. In the National League, the Brooklyn Dodgers won the pennant. The two teams met in the World Series.

The clubs were evenly matched. Cleveland won the first game, 3–1, then Brooklyn won the next two, 3–0, and 2–1. In game four, the Indians tied the Series at two games each with a 5–1 win.

The teams faced off for game five on October 10 in Cleveland. The Indians were confident. Their best pitcher, thirty-one game winner Jim Bagby, was scheduled to pitch.

Bill Wambsganss had gotten off to a slow start in the Series, failing to get a hit in the first three games. But in game four, he'd collected two hits and scored two important runs. Plus, at second base, he'd been playing good ball. And Wambsganss knew that what he did on the field was just as important to his team as what he did in the batter's box. He felt good going into the fifth game of the Series.

In the first inning of game five, Cleveland leadoff hitter Charlie Jamieson singled off Brooklyn starting pitcher Burleigh Grimes. Batting second, Bill Wambsganss got a pitch he liked and slammed it into left field for another hit. Indian center fielder Tris Speaker then bunted to load the bases.

Cleanup hitter Elmer Smith drove the ball over the right field fence for a grand-slam home run — the first ever in World Series history. It brought Cleveland fans to their feet and gave the Indians a quick 4–0 lead.

Cleveland scored three more runs in the fourth to increase their lead to seven runs. It looked as if the Indians were going to win big.

But the Dodgers didn't give up. They knew that everything could change with one swing of the bat.

Leading off the fifth inning, second baseman Pete Kilduff singled to left field off Jim Bagby. Then catcher Otto Miller followed with another base hit. With no outs, the Dodgers had men on first and second.

The Cleveland crowd suddenly turned quiet. Pitcher Jim Bagby was in trouble. If the Dodgers got a few more base hits, the Indians' seven-run lead could evaporate in a hurry.

Pitcher Clarence Mitchell stepped up to bat for Brooklyn.

At second base, Bill Wambsganss was ready. Despite Cleveland's big lead, he knew this was no time to relax. One mistake could lead to a big inning for the opposing team.

Wambsganss considered the situation. Since the Dodgers were behind by seven runs, he figured they probably wouldn't try a special play, such as a bunt or a hit-and-run. They needed to close up the score, and trying to scratch out a single run by taking a chance with a special play didn't make much sense.

The runner at second could probably score on a

base hit to the outfield. That would be the way for them to go. But if Wambsganss could knock the ball down before it went past him, he might be able to prevent a run. With that in mind, Wambsganss moved a few steps deeper at second base. If at all possible, he wanted to keep the ball in the infield.

Then Wambsganss looked at the batter. Clarence Mitchell was a left-handed hitter. That meant he was more likely to hit the ball to the right side of the infield. Although Wambsganss knew a double play would help his team, he knew it was more important to simply keep the ball in the infield and prevent the run. If I take another step back, he thought, I can still keep the ball in the infield, even if Mitchell hits it to my left. He took another step back.

Wambsganss made all these decisions in just a few seconds. He stood at the edge of the outfield grass and pounded his glove, then crouched over, ready for anything.

Pitcher Jim Bagby checked the runners, then stepped toward the plate and threw a fastball.

Mitchell swung and hit the ball on a sharp line just to the right side of second base.

If Bill Wambsganss had been playing in his usual

position, he wouldn't have had a chance at the ball; it would have been past him before he reacted. If he had been playing Mitchell to pull, the hit would have been too far to his right. But by playing a few steps deeper than usual, Wambsganss had given himself just a little more time.

At the crack of the bat, Wambsganss started running to his right. Kilduff, on second, and Miller, on first, heard the sound of the ball meeting the bat, put their heads down, and started running. The drive sounded like a base hit.

Wambsganss took only two or three steps, then instinctively jumped for the ball. He stretched his left arm across his body and turned his glove to backhand the ball.

At the top of his leap, he hung for a moment, his glove wide open.

Smack! The ball struck his mitt.

As Wambsganss hit the ground after making the catch, he saw the ball peeking over the edge of his glove. He stumbled a little as his momentum carried him toward second base, but he made sure to cover the ball with his bare hand so it wouldn't fall out.

Kilduff was still running toward third. Miller was

still running toward second. But Mitchell had taken only a few steps toward first when the home plate umpire raised his hand and called him out.

One out. But Wambsganss wasn't finished yet.

When he regained control of his body, he saw second base just ahead of him and to the left. He also saw Kilduff still racing toward third, his back to second.

Wambsganss ran for second base. Kilduff didn't have a chance. Wambsganss stepped on the bag, doubling him off.

Two outs. But Wambsganss still wasn't finished.

Otto Miller was still running toward second. When he looked up, he saw Wambsganss standing on the base, holding the ball.

Miller tried to stop and turn around. He couldn't. He was already too close to second base. He just stood there, his mouth wide open with surprise.

Wambsganss took two steps toward the bewildered Miller and touched the ball to his shoulder. Then he started running toward the dugout.

After a few seconds, the other Indian fielders started to trot off, too.

The crowd, which had cheered loudly when Wambsganss had caught Mitchell's line drive, fell quiet. They weren't quite sure what had just happened.

On third base, Kilduff looked around, confused. The umpire near third base helped him understand. He stuck his thumb out and raised it in the air.

"You're out!" he said.

Miller still stood frozen just a few feet off second. The umpire near second base stuck his thumb out and thrust his arm into the air.

"You're out!" he said.

Finally a few people in the crowd figured out what Wambsganss had done. They started to clap and cheer, then a few more joined in. In a few seconds, everyone in the stands was on their feet, roaring and waving their hats in the air.

It was a triple play!

That was rare enough. Triple plays don't happen very often. But this was something special.

This was an *unassisted* triple play! Bill Wambsganss had made all three outs himself!

In the entire history of major league baseball up to that time, only one other player had ever made an unassisted triple play. And no one had ever made such a play in the World Series. But Bill Wambsganss did. Because he was ready.

The Dodgers were done. Cleveland won the game 8–1 and took the Series the next day. Bill Wambsganss played another six years in the major leagues and then retired. He never played in another World Series, and he never made another unassisted triple play.

Nearly fifty years later, writer Lawrence Ritter asked Bill Wambsganss about the play. "It's a funny thing," he said. "I played in the big leagues for thirteen years, and the only thing anyone seems to remember is that I once made an unassisted triple play in a World Series. Many people don't even remember the team I was on, or the position I played, or anything. Just Wambsganss: unassisted triple play."

That's right — just remember the name: Wambsganss, the man who was ready.

BABE RUTH
"That's All For Me Today"

"Oomph!"

Babe Ruth grunted as he swung at the pitch and missed. He twisted around in the batter's box and nearly fell over. A murmur went through the crowd at Pittsburgh's Forbes Field. A few fans tittered and laughed as the Babe regained his balance. But most fans just looked at each other, then shook their heads knowingly.

"The poor guy," said one fan to another. "He really used to be something, you know?"

His companion nodded in agreement.

"Yep," he replied, "there never was a player like the old Bambino."

"Think we should go to tomorrow's game?" the first man asked.

"Sure," said his friend. "It'll probably be the last chance we'll ever have to see the Babe."

From 1920 through 1932, while playing for the New York Yankees in the American League, Babe Ruth was perhaps the greatest player in baseball history. He hit more home runs than any other batter. But people admired Ruth for more than his home runs. He really enjoyed the game. He was as enthusiastic as a big, overgrown kid.

When Ruth ran around the bases after hitting a homer, he would look up at the crowd with his wide, moon-shaped face, waving his cap and laughing. Even when he struck out, he was entertaining. People treated Ruth like some lovable cartoon character. He was the greatest, and people loved him for it.

But by the beginning of the 1935 season, Babe Ruth was beginning to show his age. He was forty years old and had not had a really big year since 1932. After the 1934 season, the Yankees released Ruth from his contract, leaving him free to sign with any team.

Only the lowly Boston Braves of the National League took a chance on him. The fans still loved him, and the Braves hoped he would draw a few thousand extra people to the ballpark. Maybe, they hoped, he could still hit a few home runs, too.

But over the first six weeks of the 1935 season, every game was a struggle for Ruth. Early in his career, he had been strong and robust. Now he was so fat he could barely run. Sometimes it looked as if he could barely walk to the plate. In the field, he waddled after routine fly balls and allowed them to fall for base hits. His batting average fell below .200, and the Braves' pitchers complained about his fielding. It made people sad to see him play.

Even so, when the Braves traveled to Pittsburgh in late May for a series against the Pirates, three times the usual number of fans turned out to see the Babe. The first two games of the series were a disappointment. Ruth made only two hits, both singles. Still, more than ten thousand fans filled the stands at spacious Forbes Field for game three, on Saturday, May 25, 1935.

Before the game, Pittsburgh's pitchers gathered in the clubhouse and discussed the Braves' hitters. When they came to Ruth, one pitcher recalled how Ruth had looked when he'd batted the day before. "Don't worry about Ruth," he said. Everyone laughed.

But Pirates pitcher Waite Hoyt had once been Ruth's teammate on the Yankees. "I wouldn't say that," he cautioned. Although the Babe was old and fat, Hoyt thought he might still be able to hit.

In the first inning, Ruth came up to bat against pitcher Red Lucas with one out and a man on second. It was a bright, sunny spring afternoon. Late-arriving fans hurried to their seats as the Babe stepped to the plate.

Lucas threw one pitch, and Ruth watched it go by for a ball. Lucas decided he'd fool Ruth by throwing a change-up.

But the Babe wasn't fooled. Far from it.

He swung and hit the ball with the fat part of his bat. It soared against the blue sky, long and deep to right field, dropping just over the fence and into the stands. A home run! Ruth trotted around the bases, his trademark smile on his face. The Braves led, 2–0.

On the Pittsburgh bench, Waite Hoyt turned and looked at the other Pirates pitchers. He just shook his head.

By the time Ruth came to bat in the third inning, the Pirates had replaced Red Lucas with pitcher Guy Bush. Again, there was one out and one man on base. The Pittsburgh fans cheered for the Babe.

Bush knew Ruth well. While playing for the Cubs in 1932, he had pitched against Ruth and the Yankees in the World Series. Facing him now, he remembered a famous home run Ruth had hit in that Series, a "called shot," which Ruth appeared to have predicted before he hit it. With that in mind, Bush pitched to Ruth carefully.

Ruth worked the count to 3 and 2. Then Bush threw a fastball on the inside of the plate.

Crack! Babe turned on the pitch and connected solidly. The ball sailed down the right field line, and Ruth stood at home plate, watching as it crashed against the facade of the upper deck, ten feet fair. Home run number two! The Braves now led 4–0.

Once again, Babe Ruth rounded the bases with a big smile on his face. The home run was the 713th of his career, more than twice as many as any other player.

But there was a reason the Braves were in last place in the National League. Their pitching was terrible. When Ruth came to bat in the fifth inning with a man on second, Pittsburgh led, 6–4.

This time Bush pitched even more carefully. He made sure he didn't throw Ruth a pitch he could pull.

But the Babe was a smart hitter. Instead of swinging for a home run, he smacked one of Bush's out-side pitches into left field for a single, knocking in a run and bringing the score to 6–5.

Then Ruth surprised everyone.

When the Braves' next batter singled, Ruth ran hard to second — and kept going! The Pittsburgh outfielder couldn't believe that fat old Babe Ruth was trying for third. He gunned the ball to the base.

Ruth and the ball arrived at third at the same time. Ruth slid and twisted away from the tag.

"Safe!" called the umpire. Several Pittsburgh play-ers argued, but the umpire was certain of his call. The fans laughed and clapped. "Who would have thought old Babe Ruth could still run the bases like that?" they asked each other. Ruth just stood on third, huffing and puffing and smiling at the crowd. He didn't score that inning, but he had given his fans another good memory.

With the score still 6–5 in the seventh inning, Ruth came up to bat with no outs and no one on base. Guy Bush didn't know what to do. He had already thrown Ruth two of his best pitches, and Ruth had homered and singled. Didn't the Babe know he was too old to hit this way?

Babe Ruth may have been old, but he was a smart player who knew how the game was played. He figured that Bush would try to get him to swing at bad pitches, so he was patient. Bush threw four times. The umpire called three of the pitches balls, one a strike.

All ten thousand fans in the stands were on their feet, cheering. They wanted the Babe to hit another home run. They knew that with the count at 3 and 1, Bush had to throw a strike.

Bush took a deep breath and went into his windup. He threw a fastball over the plate.

Babe Ruth turned back slightly, then swung his huge bat with all his might.

BOOM! A sound unlike any other echoed through the park as the ball met the Babe's bat. Like a rocket, the ball soared toward right field.

Ruth stood at home plate, watching as the ball continued to rise. It sailed high and deep and long, then finally disappeared over the roof of the double-decked stands in right field.

A block away, a young boy was cutting through a vacant lot when he heard the crowd roaring from the ballpark. He looked toward Forbes Field and wondered what all the racket was about. Just then, he heard a loud thump, then another, then saw a baseball bounding toward him off the roof of a house.

The boy reached down and picked up the ball. Printed on it were the words OFFICIAL NATIONAL LEAGUE BASEBALL.

The boy looked back toward Forbes Field. His eyes grew wide. He gulped.

Gosh, he thought, that must've been some home run.

Meanwhile, the crowd at the ballpark was going nuts. Old Babe Ruth had just hit his *third* home run of the game, and this home run had gone farther than any they had ever seen before. No batter had *ever* hit a ball out of Forbes Field before.

Ruth grinned and waved as he rounded the bases, happier than he had been all season. As he crossed home plate, he took off his cap and waved it to the crowd; then he trotted to the dugout. When he got to the bench, he sat down, turned to his manager, and said between deep breaths, "That's all for me today."

Ruth's home run tied the score, 6–6, but unfortunately the Braves couldn't beat Pittsburgh. They lost, 11–7, but hardly anyone cared. After the game, all anyone talked about was Babe Ruth.

One of the ushers from the ballpark, a man named Gus Miller, went looking for the third home-run ball after the game. A fan told him it had landed on the roof of a house across the street, bounced off the roof of another house, and finally landed in an empty lot, where he saw a boy pick it up and run off. Miller went to the spot and measured it. According to Miller, the ball had traveled six hundred feet!

Babe Ruth wanted to retire after the game. He wanted to quit on top. But he didn't. "I can't," he told his wife. "I promised the fans I'd play." In Cincinnati and Philadelphia, where the Braves played next, fans had planned special celebrations to honor him. Ruth didn't want to let them down.

He played one last week, hitting no home runs, then retired. The ball he hit over the roof of Forbes Field was the 714th, and last, home run of his career. His home run record stood until 1974, when it was broken by Henry Aaron, who hit 755 home runs.

Years later, someone asked Guy Bush about Ruth's 714th home run. "I never saw a ball hit so hard, before or since," replied Bush. "Babe was fat and old, but he still had that great swing. I can't forget that last one. It's probably still going."

WILLIE MAYS
The Finest Catch Ever

More than fifty thousand baseball fans pushed, shoved, and wedged their way into the Polo Grounds one fine early autumn afternoon — September 29, 1954 — to see the first game of the World Series between the New York Giants and the Cleveland Indians. Three hours and eleven minutes later, they left the ballpark convinced that they had seen the most remarkable catch in baseball history.

For seven innings, Bob Lemon, pitcher of the American League champion Cleveland Indians, battled against Sal Maglie of the National League champion New York Giants. In the first inning, Maglie hit leadoff batter Al Smith, then gave up a single to Bobby Avila, the American League's batting champion. But after the next two hitters popped up, it looked as though the runners wouldn't make it across home plate.

Then Vic Wertz, the Indians' big, slugging first baseman, came up to bat. He pulled a triple down the right field line, scoring both Smith and Avila to put the Indians ahead, 2–0.

That score held until the Giants tied up the game in the third inning. In the next several innings, Maglie and Lemon each gave up a few hits but no runs. Only a solid double from the powerful Wertz even threatened to change the score.

Then, in the top of the eighth, Maglie began to tire. Giants manager Leo Durocher was taking no chances. He motioned to the bull pen and had left-handed pitcher Don Liddle start to warm up.

Outfielder Larry Doby led off for Cleveland. Doby knew that Maglie was running out of steam, and he waited patiently for a strike. Maglie was so tired, he could hardly throw the ball over the plate. Doby walked.

Third baseman Al Rosen was up next, with slugger Vic Wertz on deck. Maglie threw one pitch, and Rosen swung.

The ball bounced sharply into the hole between second and third. New York shortstop Alvin Dark raced to his right, stuck out his bare hand, and tried to catch the ball, but it spun away. Doby pulled into second as Rosen raced to first. Both men were safe.

Giants manager Leo Durocher sighed, turned to pitching coach Freddie Fitzsimmons, and said, "He's all through. Bring in the left-hander." Fitzsimmons asked the umpire to call time out and walked onto the field.

Fitzsimmons walked slowly out to the mound, his lengthening shadow trailing behind him. When he reached the pitcher's mound, he dawdled for a moment, giving Liddle the chance to throw a few more precious pitches in the pen. Then he took the ball from Maglie and said, "Vic Wertz has been killing you. We're bringing in the left-hander."

Fitzsimmons waved toward the bull pen. Maglie walked to the Giants' dugout beyond the first base line, his head down. The team's fans cheered his effort.

Liddle trotted in and took the ball from Fitzsimmons without a word. As Fitzsimmons walked off, Liddle quickly threw a few warm-up tosses to catcher Wes Westrum, then nodded that he was ready. The plate umpire yelled, "Play ball!"

Vic Wertz stepped into the batter's box along the first base side of home plate. He ground his back foot into the dirt and looked menacingly out at Liddle. Wertz's earlier hits had made him confident.

The catcher remembered that Wertz's other hits had been off fastballs. Westrum signaled for a curve.

Liddle wound up and spun the ball toward the plate. It arrived letter-high. It did not curve.

Vic Wertz rocked back, gauged the pitch, and swung as hard as he could.

The bat made a sharp crack like a thunderbolt as it struck the ball.

The ball took off on a low, hard line toward the outfield just to the right of second base.

Liddle spun around on the mound to follow the ball on its flight. Rosen and Doby started their dash around the bases. Wertz dropped his bat and took a step toward first.

New York Giants center fielder Willie Mays had already taken *two* steps. He looked at the ball once, turned, and ran full speed toward the distant fence.

The Polo Grounds was one of the biggest ballparks in the major leagues. Although it was only 279 feet down the left field line and 257 feet to right, the outfield fences curved back sharply. It was nearly four hundred feet to the fence in both left and right center, so far from home plate that the bull pens were actually on the field, tucked against the wall. In center field, the fence was 460 feet away from home, so far away that no one had ever hit a home run to dead center field.

The crowd jumped to its feet and watched the ball. At first it didn't seem to have been hit very hard. A few Indians fans gasped as it kept soaring, but the Giants fans weren't worried. They knew there were very few balls hit to center field that Willie Mays could not catch.

The ball sailed through the crisp autumn air, only twenty or thirty feet above the ground. But unlike so many other balls hit to the outfield, this one did not slow down and drop back to earth. As the ball passed from the infield to the outfield, it continued to rise.

In center field, Willie Mays kept running.

On the Giants bench, manager Leo Durocher stood with one foot on the dugout steps. When he'd heard the crack of the bat, he had stepped up, squinting into the deep blue sky, searching for the ball.

Big Vic Wertz, lumbering toward first base, knew he had hit the ball hard. He thought it might be a home run. At the very least, he knew the hit was going to go for extra bases. He wanted to round first base at full speed.

In center field, Willie Mays kept running.

Meanwhile Giants shortstop Alvin Dark sprinted toward the outfield. His baseball instincts told him to move to the cutoff position. His common sense told him it wouldn't matter, though. He thought, That ball is not going to be caught.

Similarly second baseman Davey Williams moved toward the bag in case there was a play. He saw Al Rosen racing ahead of him toward the base.

In center field, Willie Mays kept running.

As the Indians' Larry Doby reached full stride between second and third, a thought came into his head. What if, just maybe, Mays caught the ball?

Doby slowed, turned his head, and looked toward the outfield.

All he saw was a bright white jersey, number 24 on the back, with a man inside it, running toward the fence.

In center field, Willie Mays kept running.

Now the ball was two hundred, two hundred fifty, three hundred feet from the plate, still only forty feet in the air. Now the crowd was standing. Now the crowd was yelling.

Larry Doby stopped between second and third and started to retreat toward second. He figured that if the ball fell in, he was still fast enough to score. If it *was* caught, he could tag up and race the throw to third.

In center field, Willie Mays kept running.

Finally the ball stopped rising and began to slow.

Al Rosen turned to cut around second base, but he saw Doby ahead of him, moving back toward second. Rosen started to brake.

Vic Wertz, running hard now, leaned toward the infield as he started to round first.

Liddle hoped. Durocher wished. The crowd dared to dream.

In center field, Willie Mays kept running.

The ball began to drop. Three hundred fifty feet from the plate, thirty feet in the air.

Larry Doby put his foot on second base, watched, and waited.

Al Rosen, watching Doby, staggered to a stop, dust rising as he dug his spikes into the infield dirt.

Alvin Dark kept running toward the outfield. Davey Williams straddled second.

In center field, Willie Mays kept running.

The ball kept going, dropping faster now as it sailed farther and farther into the outfield. Four hundred feet away and twenty feet from the ground.

Four hundred thirty feet away and ten feet from the ground. Four hundred fifty feet away . . .

Everyone in the crowd was on their feet, on tip-toes, holding on to the fan in the next seat for balance, craning their necks and hoping.

In center field, Willie Mays kept running.

He stretched his legs out, tilted his head back, reached his arms toward the sky, and stuck his glove into the air.

He saw the ball dropping over his head. Legs pumping, Mays stretched out his arms as far as he could — and caught the ball!

The crowd went wild. On the field, Larry Doby tagged up and sprinted toward third. Al Rosen turned and ran back toward first. Vic Wertz slowed to a jog.

Willie Mays skidded to a stop, the outfield fence looming high just in front of him. He spun around, his cap falling off, and hurled the ball so hard toward the infield that he fell to the ground.

Alvin Dark had waved for the ball, but Mays's throw sailed over his head. Larry Doby pulled up at third. Davey Williams gathered in Mays's throw at second. Al Rosen pulled into first.

Doby was safe at third. Rosen was safe at first.

Vic Wertz was out. He jogged back to the Indians' dugout.

Willie Mays stood up, picked up his cap, placed it back on his head, and started to walk back to where he'd started.

All 52,751 fans cheered, clapped, whistled, and roared.

It was still the eighth inning. And thanks to Mays's catch, the game was still tied, 2–2.

The amazing event had taken place in only three or four seconds.

The Indians didn't score that inning. The next hitter walked to load the bases, but the next man struck out, and the third flew out to left field.

The Giants couldn't score either. At the bottom of the ninth, the score was still tied 2–2, so the game entered extra innings. The crowd didn't have long to wait for the final outcome. A three-run homer by pinch hitter Dusty Rhodes in the tenth won the game for the Giants, 5–2.

After the game, everyone congratulated Rhodes for his big home run. But all anyone could talk about was Willie Mays.

Vic Wertz said, "That's the longest drive I ever hit in my life. I thought it was in the bleachers. Honest."

Indians manager Al Lopez said, "That catch was the best I ever saw. The best I *ever* saw."

After watching the game from the press box, Brooklyn Dodgers general manager Branch Rickey sent Willie Mays a note. Sitting in front of his locker, Mays carefully opened the small piece of paper. It read, *That was the finest catch I have ever seen, and the finest I ever hope to see*. Mays smiled.

Many people still feel the same way Rickey and Lopez did. They remember seeing Willie Mays. In center field. Running and reaching and stretching. Making the catch.

TED WILLIAMS
The Greatest Hitter's
Last At Bat

While Ted Williams was growing up in San Diego, he spent all his free time playing baseball. Each day, as soon as school was over, Ted rushed to North Park, a local playground, and talked a friend into playing a game Ted called Big League. One boy would stand in front of a wire backstop and pitch a ball to the other, who hit the ball back toward the screen.

Ted did not like being the pitcher. All he wanted to do was hit. After taking only a few swings, Ted did not even notice the wire backstop behind the pitcher. Ted imagined he was in the major leagues. The backstop became a ballpark full of people. The sound of the wind blowing across the playground became the cheers of thousands of fans. His friend throwing the baseball became the fastest, meanest pitcher in the major leagues. And Ted became the greatest hitter in baseball history.

32

Hitting a baseball was all Ted Williams thought about. When he joined the Boston Red Sox as a twenty-year-old rookie, in 1939, Williams told his teammates that he had one dream. "Someday," he said, "when I walk down the street, I want people to say, 'There goes the greatest hitter who ever lived.'"

By the time Ted Williams was ready to retire from baseball, in 1960, his dream had come true. For over twenty years, the left-handed-hitting Boston Red Sox left fielder was one of the greatest batters in the history of baseball. In all but one season, Williams hit over .300. He won the American League batting title six times. In 1941, he hit .406, the last major league player to hit above .400. He led the American League in batting average, home runs, and runs batted in — the triple crown — twice. He hit more than five hundred home runs, and his career batting average was .344.

But even Ted Williams couldn't play forever. Late in the 1960 season, he decided to retire from baseball at the end of the season. He would be forty-two years old.

The Red Sox were scheduled to play their last home game of the year against the Baltimore Orioles on September 28. Although the team still had to play three more games in New York to finish the season, Ted Williams wanted to play his last game at Fenway Park.

Williams didn't want anyone to make a fuss about his last game. But the mayor of Boston declared September 28 "Ted Williams Day."

And as Williams sat in the locker room getting dressed before the game, sportswriters came up to him and asked how it felt to retire. Williams shooed them away. He didn't want to answer any questions. He just wanted to play baseball one more time.

Outside Fenway Park, small groups of fans trickled out of the subway stop. As they hurried down the street toward the ballpark, they zipped their jackets and looked up at the sky. The day was cool and cloudy, and a damp breeze was blowing in off Boston Harbor.

The damp weather kept many fans away from the game. Others didn't show up because they refused to believe that Ted Williams would ever quit playing baseball. By the time the game was scheduled to start, Fenway Park was barely half full.

Just before the game, the Red Sox held a brief ceremony on the field to honor Williams. The Red Sox television announcer, Curt Gowdy, stood on the field near home plate in a long coat and spoke into a large microphone on a stand.

"As we all know," he said, "this is the final game for — in my opinion and most of yours — the greatest hitter who ever lived, Ted Williams."

Gowdy told stories about Williams's career, and the crowd cheered as they remembered the way Williams looked when he swung the bat — loose and fast, as though it was all he ever wanted to do.

Gowdy ended his remarks by saying, "I don't think we'll see another one like him."

Williams walked up to the microphone and looked around as everyone in the stands stood up and applauded. He was happy and sad all at the same time. He, too, remembered the home runs and waving his cap to the crowd, but he also remembered being booed when he didn't get a hit and arguing with sportswriters when they wrote something he didn't think was fair. Williams was going to miss playing baseball, but he was not going to miss talking with sportswriters or being booed.

The crowd finally hushed as Williams started to speak. He had not written a speech. He just spoke from his heart.

"Baseball has been the most wonderful thing in

my life," he said. "If I were starting over again and someone asked me where is the one place I would like to play, I would want it to be in Boston, with the greatest fans in America. Thank you."

The crowd cheered some more as Ted Williams put his head down and walked quickly to the bench. He looked up once and winked, then ducked into the dugout and waited for the game to begin.

In the first inning, Williams came to bat with his teammate Willie Tasby on first base. On the mound for the Baltimore Orioles was Steve Barber. He was only twenty-one years old. When Ted Williams began his major league career, Barber had been an infant.

Williams stood at bat and tried to concentrate. He always thought it was more difficult facing a pitcher the first few times, and he had not hit against Barber very many times before. All he knew was that Barber threw fast. And wild.

Williams decided to be patient. He thought Barber would probably be nervous. He would wait for a good pitch. He always refused to swing unless the pitch was a strike.

Barber threw four pitches. Each time, Williams stood absolutely still in the batter's box, his bat cocked behind his ear, as the ball approached the plate. As it zipped past him, Williams turned his head and followed it into the catcher's glove. He knew, even before the umpire made his call, that each pitch was a ball. He went to first base with a walk, and Tasby trotted to second.

Red Sox catcher Jim Pagliaroni came up next. Barber did not want to walk another hitter and threw the ball over the plate. Pagliaroni singled, and Willie Tasby scored. Williams moved to second.

Then the Red Sox's Lu Clinton stepped to the plate. Barber threw a fastball, but it got past the catcher and dribbled away. Williams raced to third.

The Orioles infielders looked over at Williams, surprised. He was forty-two years old. Who could have expected him to take the extra base? But they didn't know Ted Williams. This was his last game, and he was going to play as well as he possibly could.

Lu Clinton hit a short fly ball to Orioles center fielder Jackie Brandt. Williams stood on third base and watched the ball settle into Brandt's glove. As soon as the ball was caught, Williams raced for home. He took the Orioles by surprise again. No one expected old Ted Williams to try to score. Brandt quickly threw the ball home. Williams slid across the plate, inches ahead of the ball.

Safe! The fans roared and laughed. Although they wanted to see Williams hit a home run, watching him run the bases as though he was twenty years old was almost as good. Even better was that now the Red Sox led, 2–0.

Williams came up to bat again in the third inning with no one on base. The Orioles had sent in a relief pitcher, Jack Fisher, who was the same age as Steve Barber.

Once again, Williams stood absolutely still in the batter's box and watched Fisher's first pitch sail past the plate. Ball one.

Fisher wound up and threw again. Again Williams stood and watched the ball go by. He figured that Fisher would also be nervous and decided he would not swing until Fisher proved to him that he could throw a strike.

Williams grimaced when the next pitch smacked into the catcher's mitt. It was a good pitch, the kind he liked. The umper yelled "Strike!" but Williams already knew that. He was thinking of the next pitch. He wanted to be ready.

He was. His body uncoiled as he swung at Fisher's next pitch. The ball rose on a line toward center field. Fisher spun around on the mound to watch the ball. Everyone in the crowd stood up to watch, thinking the same thought: Would Ted Williams hit a home run in his last game?

But a moment later, they began to sit again. Orioles center fielder Jackie Brandt drifted back a few steps and settled under the fly ball. Ted had hit the ball deep, but the fence in center field was more than four hundred feet away from the plate. Brandt caught the ball for an easy out, and the last cheers were drowned out by a disappointing groan.

As Williams ran back to the dugout, the public address announcer told the crowd that the Red Sox would retire his uniform number, 9, after the game.

As the announcer's words echoed off the left field fence, the fans in the stands looked at one another and started to shake their heads. They finally realized this really was Williams's last game. They would get to see him hit only once or twice more.

They paid little attention to the rest of the game even though Baltimore rallied to take a 3–2 lead. Everyone was waiting for Ted Williams to come to bat again.

With two outs in the fifth inning, Williams slowly

walked to the plate for the third time. Jack Fisher was still pitching. Williams liked facing a pitcher several times in a game. Every time at bat, he learned something, like how fast the pitcher threw, what pitches he liked, and how the ball moved. The more he learned, the better he hit. Now he figured he had the advantage.

Fisher threw the ball, and Williams liked what he saw. He swung, a little earlier this time, pulling the ball high and deep to right field, where the fence was not quite so far away. As Williams ran from the batter's box down the first base line, his eyes searched the gray sky for the ball. Once again, the fans at Fenway Park jumped to their feet.

Orioles right fielder Al Pilarcik looked up at the ball and ran back toward the low fence in front of the Red Sox bull pen. The sign on the fence read 380 FT. Up in the sky, the ball was a small black dot. The outfielder waited with his back against the fence.

Williams ran around first base, still watching the ball as it dropped from the sky. But just as the crowd started to roar, Pilarcik raised his glove in front of his face and caught the fly. The crowd moaned and sat back down. Williams looked away, then slowed to a jog, and finally came to a stop. He stood on the field and looked at the ground as he waited for a teammate to bring him his glove. He was disappointed. He had hit the ball hard, but not hard enough for a home run.

The clouds thickened, and the lights were turned on at Fenway Park in the sixth inning. But that didn't help the Red Sox. Entering the eighth inning, Baltimore led, 4–2.

Red Sox leadoff batter Willie Tasby stepped from the dugout to start the inning, and the crowd started to roar. But they were not cheering Willie Tasby. They knew Ted Williams would bat next.

Tasby hit a ground ball to the shortstop, and before the shortstop even fielded the ball and threw to first base for the out, the crowd started cheering again, louder and longer than they had cheered all day. Ted Williams was coming to bat one more time.

Everyone in the stands knew this would be the last time Ted Williams would take his stance at the plate. The hot dog vendors stopped and set down their trays. No one left their seat to get a soft drink. The stands underneath the park were empty. Everyone was watching Ted Williams.

As Williams stood in the batter's box, the crowd clapped and cheered for two full minutes. Williams swung his bat and tried to concentrate.

Twice before in his career, he had come to the plate unsure if he would ever get to bat again. In 1952 he was drafted into military service to fight in the Korean War. He didn't know if he would ever play baseball again. Then, at the end of the 1954 season, he had planned to retire, but he later changed his mind. Each time, thinking he might never bat again, he had hit a home run.

Jack Fisher stood on the mound and waited for the cheering to stop before he toed the rubber and took the sign from the Orioles catcher. He knew it was Ted Williams's last at bat, but he wasn't going to do him any favors. Fisher wanted to get Williams out and win the ball game.

Jack Fisher's first pitch was low. Williams didn't swing. He just watched the ball smack into the catcher's glove and waited for the umpire to signal a ball. He did.

Fisher wound up and threw again. As the ball left his hand, the crowd stopped cheering. Everyone stood absolutely still and silent, waiting to see what would happen next.

Williams knew he could hit Fisher's pitches. His second time up, he had tried to be a little quicker than he'd been the first time, pulling the ball to right center. This time, he tried to swing even quicker still.

Fisher's pitch crossed the plate. Williams stepped toward it. The bat came off his shoulder and ripped across the plate as he turned into the pitch and swung.

He missed. He spun around awkwardly in the batter's box as the catcher flipped the ball back to Fisher. Everyone in the crowd knew what Williams was trying to do. He was trying to hit a home run. But was he trying too hard?

Fisher wound up again. Williams reminded himself to make sure the pitch was good and not to swing too hard, but to swing fast.

The ball came in waist-high and over the middle of the plate.

Ted Williams swung. This time he didn't miss. Everyone in the ballpark heard the loud *crack* as his bat met the ball.

The ball rose on a line to right center field. This time the fans didn't wait to cheer. They immediately started jumping up and down and yelling. Orioles right fielder Al Pilarcik turned and started to run back after the ball but stopped. Ted Williams was the only person moving on the entire field.

The ball sailed over the fence and bounced off the roof of the canopy over the Red Sox bench in the bull pen.

Home run!

Ted looked down at the ground and ran around the bases. The crowd cheered and people tossed hot dog wrappers and empty soda cups into the air. Ted didn't even look up as he crossed the plate, shook teammate Jim Pagliaroni's hand, and raced into the dugout. His teammates clapped him on the back and applauded.

Then the crowd started chanting, "WE WANT TED. WE WANT TED. WE WANT TED." But Williams stayed in the dugout. His teammates wanted him to go on the field and tip his hat to the crowd, but he refused. He wanted to leave people with a memory. He wanted them to remember his last swing and the ball sailing through the air and dropping over the fence. He wanted them to remember Ted Williams circling the bases for a home run.

The Red Sox made three quick outs, but no one in the stands noticed. They were still talking about Ted Williams. They started to cheer again as they saw him running out to left field. Then they saw another player run to replace him, giving them one last chance to cheer for Williams as he ran back in. He stepped on first base, dashed into the dugout, then went down the runway to the locker room.

As the crowd in Fenway Park watched Ted Williams run off the field for the last time, they told each other, "There goes the greatest hitter that ever lived." Ted Williams's dream had come true.

REGGIE JACKSON
Three Pitches,
Three Swings . . .

"Reggie, Reggie, Reggie!"

As Reggie Jackson stepped up to bat for the Yankees in the eighth inning of game five of the 1977 World Series, he heard the fans chanting his name. It was a familiar sound, but didn't always mean the same thing.

Sometimes the chant meant Jackson had done something the crowd liked. But at other times, the chant was a jeer meant to remind him that he had played poorly. This time, the pro-Dodger crowd in Los Angeles was jeering him.

Although the Yankees were ahead in the World Series, they were losing game five. The Dodgers led 10–3 when Reggie Jackson came to bat in the eighth inning.

On the mound, Dodgers pitcher Don Sutton was relaxed. He stared down at the left-handed-hitting

46

Jackson, who stood in the batter's box wiggling the bat behind his ear. Sutton wound up and threw a fastball.

Wham! Jackson uncoiled and sent the ball on a low line drive toward right field. Dodgers outfielder Lee Lacy turned around and started after the ball but stopped. It dropped just over the fence for a home run.

As Jackson quickly circled the bases to make the score 10–4, the remaining Dodgers fans stopped chanting his name. Although Jackson's home run came too late to help the Yankees, Dodgers fans still didn't like it. The Dodgers won, 10–4.

The 1977 season had been a rocky one for Reggie Jackson. In the spring, he had signed with the Yankees as a highly paid free agent. Everyone — including himself — expected him to lead the Yankees to the World Series.

In an interview before the season started, Jackson had said, "You know this team, it all flows from me. I've got to keep it all going. I'm the straw that stirs the drink. It all comes back to me."

Jackson hadn't meant to offend anyone with his comments, but many of his teammates thought he was a braggart. They knew he was one of the greatest sluggers in the game. But New York had won the American League pennant without him the year before. The Yankees were already a good team.

Jackson had gotten off to a bad start with his new teammates. As the season progressed, the situation worsened. For all his confident statements, he played poorly. The crowd's cheers turned to jeers.

Then, in mid-June, he misplayed a ball hit to the outfield into a double. Yankee manager Billy Martin yanked him from the lineup in the middle of the game.

Jackson was so furious, he couldn't hold his anger back. He yelled at Billy Martin, and Martin yelled back. The two men nearly got into a fight. In the end, Jackson was fined. He spent the next two months in and out of the Yankee lineup. When he played, he performed poorly. The team soon fell to third place and was in danger of dropping out of the pennant race.

The conflict between Martin and Jackson was hurting the team. So, in early August, Yankee owner George Steinbrenner met with both men. They decided to end the feud. Jackson would play, and bat cleanup, for the rest of the season.

As soon as he was solidly back in the lineup, Jackson started hitting again. For the next two months, he and the Yankees were on fire. New York surged past both Boston and Baltimore to win the American League's Eastern Division. Jackson finished the regular season with thirty-two home runs and a team-high 110 RBIs. The "Reggie" chant was a cheer again.

But it was not to remain so for long. In the first five games of the American League championship against the Kansas City Royals, Jackson had only one hit. Billy Martin benched him.

Everyone expected Jackson to explode with anger again. But he didn't. And when Martin asked him to pinch-hit later in the same game, Jackson responded with an RBI single. The Yankees won, 5–3, defeating the Royals to win the pennant.

With the World Series right around the corner, Jackson made it clear that he was ready to show the Yankees and their fans what he was made of.

He did. In the World Series, Jackson went back into the starting lineup, and the Yankees played well. After five games they led the Dodgers three games to two. In both game four and game five, Jackson had hit a home run. Despite the jeers from Dodgers fans, Jackson felt like himself again.

The Series returned to New York on October 18

for game six. In batting practice, Jackson sent pitch after pitch into the stands. Other players just stopped and watched. As Jackson later described in his autobiography, "The baseball looked like a volleyball to me." After batting practice, Yankee second baseman Willie Randolph went up to Jackson, smiled, and said, "Would you do us all a favor and save some of that?"

Jackson laughed. "There's more where that came from," he said. He could hardly contain himself before the start of the game. "I feel great," he blurted out to a teammate.

The Dodgers jumped out to a quick 2–0 lead in the first inning. Jackson was first up at the start of the second.

Dodgers pitcher Burt Hooton worked Jackson carefully. Most pitchers either threw the ball far inside on Jackson, trying to jam him, or threw to the outside corner, where he couldn't reach the ball. Hooton tried to do both, but he either threw the ball too far in or too far outside. Jackson looked at four pitches and walked.

Then Yankee first baseman Chris Chambliss homered. Jackson and Chambliss scored, and the game was tied, 2–2. But the Dodgers scored a single run in the third to go ahead again, 3–2.

In the fourth, Yankee catcher Thurman Munson led off with a single. Reggie Jackson stepped to the plate.

Hooton wound up and threw a fastball down the middle of the plate.

To Jackson, it looked as big as a volleyball. And volleyballs are easy to hit.

Boom!

The ball streaked to right field and landed in the grandstand for a home run so quickly that Jackson had hardly moved from the batter's box before it fell. One pitch. One swing. One home run.

Suddenly the Yankees led, 4–3. The crowd at Yankee Stadium stood on its feet and cheered. As Jackson loped around the bases, they started to chant his name.

"Reggie! Reggie! Reggie!"

Dodgers manager Tommy Lasorda pulled Burt Hooton and replaced him with relief pitcher Elias Sosa. The Yankees scored once more in the fourth, increasing their lead to 5–3.

Jackson was scheduled to be up fourth in the fifth inning. As leadoff hitter Mickey Rivers stepped into the batter's box, Jackson strolled the length of the dugout and grabbed his bat. He knew he was going to get a chance to hit, and he could hardly wait.

Rivers singled, but the next two Yankees made outs. Then Reggie Jackson stepped to the plate once again.

Sosa hoped to catch Jackson off guard. His catcher called for a fastball and crouched behind the plate with his glove on the outside corner.

Jackson was ready. As soon as the ball left Sosa's hand, he knew it was a fastball. It looked as big as a volleyball again.

Jackson swung from his heels and pulled the outside pitch down the right field line. If anything, he hit this ball even harder than his home run off Hooton the inning before.

The ball streaked down the right field line and slammed into the box seats just over the fence.

One pitch, one swing, and one more home run for Reggie Jackson.

Jackson romped around the bases with a big grin on his face. The Yankee Stadium crowd was delirious. The problems he had faced earlier in the year washed away as the chant of "Reggie, Reggie, Reggie" grew louder.

The Dodgers were numb. Yankee starting pitcher Mike Torrez pitched better each inning. Entering the last of the eighth, the Yankees still led, 7–3.

Charlie Hough, the fourth pitcher of the game for

the Dodgers, took the mound. Reggie Jackson led off for the Yankees.

When Jackson emerged from the Yankee dugout, all 56,407 fans in Yankee Stadium stood on their feet, cheering and chanting, "Reggie, Reggie, Reggie," over and over again. Reggie Jackson dug into the batter's box, adjusted his batting helmet, and looked out at Hough.

Hough threw knuckleballs. The pitch wasn't thrown very fast, but the ball moved a lot. Jackson knew it was important to wait as long as possible on the pitch.

Hough wound up and threw.

Jackson waited, watching the ball dance toward the plate.

Tonight, it didn't matter what Hough threw or where he threw it. The ball looked big to Reggie Jackson.

He exploded with a mighty swing, spinning around in the batter's box and nearly dropping to his knees with the effort.

Crack!

The ball sailed into the night, one bright speck soaring through the air, high and deep toward center field.

The Dodgers center fielder didn't even bother to

move. Jackson didn't even bother to run. Everyone in Yankee Stadium just stood and watched.

The ball soared over the fence in dead center field and slammed against the tarpaulin that covered the bleachers some 450 feet from home plate.

When the ball finally landed, Jackson threw his bat to the ground and started to half run, half hop toward first base.

One last pitch. One last swing. One more home run for Reggie Jackson!

With each step he took around the bases, he heard the chant of "Reggie!" echo through the stadium. Those same words flashed on the center field scoreboard. Reggie smiled and danced around the bases, jumped on home plate with both feet, then collapsed into the arms of his teammates before disappearing into the Yankee dugout.

At that moment the crowd began to realize exactly what Jackson had done.

He had come to bat four times. He had swung at exactly three pitches. He had hit three home runs!

Jackson stepped from the dugout several times and waved his cap at the crowd over and over again. The fans just couldn't seem to stop cheering him.

The Series was all but over. The Dodgers scored a

meaningless run in the ninth, but when the Yankees won the game, 8–4, they took the Series, four games to two.

After the game, a sportswriter remembered that Jackson had hit a home run with his last swing in game five. That meant he had hit four homers on four consecutive swings. That plus his game four homer, gave him a total of five home runs in the World Series! No one, not even Babe Ruth, had done that before.

Even the Dodgers were in awe. After the game, Dodgers manager Tommy Lasorda said, "That's the greatest performance I have ever seen. That is the greatest performance I will *ever* see."

Dodgers first baseman Steve Garvey agreed. He told one sportswriter, "I must admit, when Reggie hit that third home run, and I was sure no one was looking, I applauded in my glove."

Three pitches, three swings, three home runs.

Reggie! Reggie! Reggie!

DAVE DRAVECKY
Back in "the Zone"

Late in the 1987 season, San Francisco Giants pitcher Dave Dravecky was undressing after a game. As he pulled his uniform shirt off, he felt for the small lump on his upper left arm. It was still there.

Dravecky had noticed the lump a few days before. Pitchers always worry about their arms and usually notice the least little difference or twinge of pain. Now Dravecky called out to Mark Letendre, the Giants' trainer.

"Hey, Mark, take a look at this little lump."

Letendre dropped the towels he was carrying and walked over to Dravecky. He rolled up the sleeve on Dravecky's undershirt and felt the small bump with his fingers. He looked up at Dravecky, shrugged, and said, "Don't worry about it."

Dravecky decided to take that advice, because in

the late summer and fall of 1987, everything was just about perfect. Dave Dravecky was in "the zone."

When Dravecky was in what he called the zone, he threw every pitch exactly where he wanted it to go. That was important, because he didn't throw the ball fast enough to get it by a hitter. He was a finesse pitcher. To win, he had to throw the ball exactly where the hitter least expected it to be.

When Dravecky was in the zone, he didn't notice the fans in the stands or the bright blue sky above Candlestick Park. He didn't care who was at bat or what the score was. All he saw was the catcher's mitt. He hardly even paid attention to the signs. The catcher would put out his glove, Dravecky would wind up, and *zip!* The ball was in the mitt.

The Giants won the National League Western Division, and in the play-offs Dravecky had pitched the best baseball of his career. He pitched twice, beating the St. Louis Cardinals 5–0 while giving up only two hits. Although he lost a heartbreaker, 1–0, when one of his teammates made an error, and the Giants eventually lost to the Cardinals, Dravecky was extremely happy with his performance.

Everything was almost perfect.

But almost perfect wasn't enough. The lump in Dravecky's arm didn't go away.

In the off-season, Dave thought about the lump again and decided to have it looked at. His doctor ordered an MRI, which is like an X ray but shows soft tissue as well and is much more detailed. During the MRI, Dravecky had to lie perfectly still in a long tube for more than an hour while the machine took a "picture" of the inside of his arm.

After looking at the MRI, the doctors told Dravecky not to worry. They thought the lump was just scar tissue from an old injury. But they told him to have it checked again in six months just to make sure.

When spring training began a few months later, Dravecky picked up right where he had left off in the play-offs, pitching well during the exhibition season. A few days before the beginning of the season, Giants manager Roger Craig, a former pitcher himself, walked up to Dravecky.

"Well, big boy," he drawled, "I'm going to give you the ball for opening day. You're my guy."

Dravecky just smiled, but inside he was so happy he wanted to jump up and down. Craig knew how much it meant to a pitcher to throw on opening day.

Dravecky was pitching well, his arm felt good, and now this. Everything seemed perfect.

Except for that small lump.

Dravecky pitched and won on opening day. After the game, he told his wife, "You know something? I think 1988 is going to be my year." Janice Dravecky smiled. She knew what he meant. Although he had been a major league pitcher for seven years, he had never won twenty games in a season. Dravecky thought 1988 was going to be the year he did just that.

But in the next few games he pitched, he couldn't seem to get loose. The ball wouldn't go where he wanted it to anymore. He was definitely not in the zone, and he couldn't seem to remember how to get back.

But he kept trying. Then his arm started to hurt, at first just a little. But soon his shoulder throbbed every time he picked up a baseball. In the middle of the season, Dravecky went on the disabled list.

Doctors re-examined his arm and decided he should undergo a minor operation. A small tendon in his shoulder had frayed and was getting stuck in the joint. That was why his arm hurt.

After the operation, Dravecky started working out,

at first just doing exercises and then throwing. His arm didn't hurt until he tried to throw hard. Then it felt like it was going to fall off. The Giants told him not to pitch anymore that season.

Dravecky had the lump on his arm examined again. This time, the doctors noticed the lump was growing.

They sent him to different doctors for more tests. Then he went to still more doctors for even more tests. These last doctors performed a biopsy on the lump. A surgeon cut a small hole in his upper arm and extracted some sample tissue of the lump.

For two days, Dave and Janice waited for the doctor to call back with the results. Finally the phone rang.

It was Janice's brother. He was a doctor himself, and he had spoken to Dave's doctor. "Dave," he said, "you have cancer. But if you have to have cancer, you have about the best kind."

Dravecky had what was known as a desmoid tumor. While it was unlikely to spread through his body, it was hard to get rid of. Doctors would have to remove not only the tumor itself but also all the muscle and bone nearby, including over half of Dravecky's deltoid muscle, one of only three muscles in the upper arm.

When Dravecky met later with his doctor, he was told the worst news yet. "Your chances of returning to professional baseball are zero," the doctor said. "With intensive therapy, you *might* be able to play catch with your son in your backyard."

Dravecky swallowed hard. As he wrote in his autobiography, he then told the doctor, "Don't think I'm going to go off into a closet and cry. I've had a great career, and I'm ready to go on to whatever is next."

He meant it. He had enjoyed his career, but he didn't think baseball was the most important thing in the world. He loved the game, but he loved his family and friends more.

Dravecky entered the hospital for the operation a few days later. But when surgeons cut into his deltoid muscle, they discovered that the tumor was growing right next to the humerus bone, in his upper arm. Concerned that the tumor might have spread into the bone, doctors froze part of the bone to kill it. They hoped this would also kill any remaining cancer cells. The bone itself would grow back, although it would be brittle for the next several months.

Doctors told Dravecky that it would be months before he could move his arm normally. It would even be difficult for him to take his wallet out of his back pocket. The muscle that made his arm move that way was just about gone.

After the operation, Dravecky started undergoing therapy. He worked hard to strengthen the remaining muscles in his arm and regain his range of motion. Then, after only a few weeks of therapy, Dravecky went into the kichen, where his wife was washing the dishes.

"Janice," he said, "watch this."

Janice Dravecky turned. Very slowly Dave reached his left arm into his back pocket and threw his wallet on the counter. Then he stood as if he was holding an imaginary baseball and slowly went through his windup. He could move his arm just as much as he could before the operation.

Janice started to cry. "I can't believe it," she said.

When Dravecky showed his doctors what he could do, they were stunned. "How can you do that?" one asked.

All Dravecky knew was that he could. It was a miracle.

"Okay," said one doctor. "Let's get you throwing."

Over the next several months, Dravecky slowly worked up to throwing a baseball. The doctors warned him that if his arm ever started to hurt, he would have to stop. First he threw a football back and forth with his brother. Ever so slowly, he increased the distance he threw. By mid-March, doctors let him throw a baseball.

Dravecky then went to spring training. Each day, he threw a little harder. Although the Gaints started their season without him, Dravecky kept working out.

In July, just nine months after his operation, he was ready. He was throwing almost as hard as he did before the operation. The Giants decided to send him to the minor leagues to see what he could do.

They sent him to their single A team in San Jose, California. He joined the club in Stockton, where San Jose was scheduled to play next.

Dravecky loved just being back in the locker room. When he looked around to his younger team-mates, he remembered what it was like when he first started playing professional baseball.

When he walked out onto the field, he felt like he had just walked into a surprise birthday party. Nearly five thousand fans had pushed their way into the tiny minor league ballpark. Everyone was cheering for him.

And as he wound up and threw his first pitch, Dravecky was in the zone again. He pitched the whole game and won.

Dravecky wanted to join the Giants immediately, but the front office still couldn't believe that he was pitching. They made him pitch twice more in the minors, once for San Jose and once for their triple A team, the Phoenix Giants.

Dave won both games.

Meanwhile the Giants were fighting for first place in the National League Western Division. Several of their pitchers were on the disabled list. So at last they called Dave Dravecky back up to the major leagues.

The Giants scheduled Dravecky to pitch on August 10 against the Cincinnati Reds at Candlestick Park, in San Francisco.

Fifteen minutes before the game, Dravecky left the Giants' clubhouse and walked up the dimly lit tunnel to the dugout. As he walked onto the field, he couldn't believe his eyes.

Photographers and sportswriters crowded onto the field. Candlestick Park was packed with people. When Dravecky stepped out of the dugout, everyone roared and cheered.

Dravecky turned to his pitching coach and asked, "What's going on?" The coach smiled. Everyone just wanted to see Dave Dravecky pitch again.

When Dravecky took the mound, he was nervous and excited at the same time. He had proven he could pitch in the minor leagues, but major league hitters were different. He would have to prove he could still pitch against the country's best players.

Dravecky wound up and threw his first pitch to Reds hitter Luis Quinones. Ball one. But the crowd cheered as if it was the last strike in the World Series.

Dravecky threw another pitch. Quinones pulled it savagely down the line. Foul.

Dravecky took a deep breath. Throwing the ball just wasn't good enough, he thought. He had to start *pitching*.

Quinones worked the count to 3 and 2. Then Dravecky threw his favorite pitch, the backdoor slider. Quinones lifted a fly to center field.

Out! The crowd gave Dravecky a standing ovation.

Suddenly Dravecky was in the zone again, just playing catch. Inning after inning the Reds went down in order as the crowd kept roaring and cheering for Dravecky.

Entering the eighth inning, Dravecky had given up only one hit and the Giants led, 4–0. But Dravecky was getting tired. The first batter, Todd Benzinger, blooped the ball just over the infield for a base hit.

The next hitter flew out, then Dravecky gave up a double to rookie Scott Madison, putting runners on second and third.

The crowd started getting nervous. They didn't want Dravecky to lose.

He pitched carefully to the next hitter, Ron Oester, who worked the count to 3 and 2. Then Dave threw the backdoor slider.

Oester swung.

He missed! Strike three! The fans jumped from their seats and started cheering again.

Dravecky was now as tired as an old dog. He wasn't throwing the ball quite where he wanted to. He was out of the zone. The Reds' next batter, Luis Quinones, hit a fly ball to left field. It landed over the fence for a home run. The Giants led by only one run, 4–3.

Dravecky felt sick for a moment, then turned his concentration toward the next hitter. He got him to ground out to the shortstop.

As Dravecky left the mound, the crowd cheered

even louder than before. Giants manager Roger Craig went up to him.

"You're finished, big guy," he said. "Go take a shower, and we'll win this one for you."

Dravecky smiled, but he didn't go take a shower. He took a seat on the bench. He had worked too hard to leave now. He wanted to watch every pitch. He wanted to see for himself that his first game back had ended in victory.

In the ninth inning, Giants relief pitcher Steve Bedrosian set down the Reds in order. The game was over. The Giants had won. Against incredible odds, Dravecky had fought his way back into the zone.

The clubhouse was bedlam. Reporters crowded around Dravecky, asking a thousand questions at once.

Dravecky held up his hand. "Before I take any more questions, it's important to give credit where credit's due." Then he thanked God for giving him the opportunity to pitch again, and he thanked his wife, his doctors, his therapists, and his teammates for their help.

"What's next?" asked another reporter.

"Anything else," said Dravecky, "is icing on the cake."

EPILOGUE

Five days after the victory over the Reds, Dravecky's left arm, still weak from where the bone had been frozen, snapped. At that moment, Dravecky knew his career was over. But as he was carried off the field on a stretcher, he sat up, head held high. Only his arm was broken, not his spirit. He had proven he could do what no one had thought possible. Less than a year later, the cancer in Dravecky's arm returned. Doctors amputated the arm to make certain the cancer would not return. Today Dave Dravecky is cancer-free.

KIRK GIBSON
"One Good Swing Left"

On the Dodgers bench, no one was smiling.

It was the end of the eighth inning of game one of the 1988 World Series, and the Los Angeles Dodgers trailed the Oakland Athletics 4–3.

Before the Series even began, nearly everyone had predicted an Oakland victory. The Dodgers were a good team, but the Athletics had stormed through the 1988 season, winning 104 games and finishing thirteen games ahead of the second place Minnesota Twins in the American League's Western Division. Then, in the League Championship Series, the A's had defeated the Boston Red Sox in four straight games.

Everyone thought Oakland was the best team in baseball. Few people believed the Dodgers stood a chance against them. In fact, some people thought the Dodgers were lucky to be in the World Series at all.

Dodger hopes dropped even lower on the eve of

69

the World Series. In the last game of the play-offs, the Dodgers' only slugger, outfielder Kirk Gibson, sprained ligaments in his right knee. He was already playing with a painful pulled hamstring in his left thigh. Dodgers doctors told manager Tommy Lasorda that it was doubtful Gibson would even be able to play in the World Series.

The Dodgers needed Gibson. They were a team built around pitching and defense. Gibson was the only strong offensive player in the Dodgers lineup. He was so important to the team that he was later named the National League's Most Valuable Player for the 1988 season. All season long, the Dodgers had looked to Gibson, and all season long he had come through. Now they would have to win without him.

In the Dodgers' clubhouse before game one, sportswriters gathered around manager Tommy Lasorda and asked him about Gibson. Gibson meanwhile was in the trainer's room, lying on a table while the team trainer carefully wrapped his thigh and knee in bandages.

Lasorda looked sadly at the writers and shook his head. "He can't do it," he lamented. "He just can't do it." Gibson wasn't even introduced to the crowd before the game.

Yet when the game started in Los Angeles on October 15, it appeared as if the Dodgers might be able to get by without Gibson after all. In the first inning, light-hitting left fielder Mickey Hatcher surprised everyone and smacked a home run to put the Dodgers ahead, 2–0.

But Dodger optimism was short-lived. In the second inning, the A's right fielder, Jose Canseco, hit a grand-slam home run. Suddenly the Athletics led, 4–2. Without Gibson, the Dodgers were going to have a hard time catching up.

But the Dodgers didn't give up. They didn't allow the A's to score again in the next four innings. Then, in the sixth inning, the Dodgers added another run, putting them within one of the A's. Neither team scored in the seventh and eighth.

Gibson sat in the Dodgers' clubhouse watching the game on television. In the eighth inning, he heard the announcer say, "Kirk Gibson, spearhead of the Dodger offense, will not see any action tonight, for sure."

Gibson stared at the TV screen and slowly stood up. He grabbed his shirt and put it on. As he buttoned the shirt, he looked over to Dodgers batboy Mitch Poole, and said, "I'll be there." Then he picked up a bat and asked Poole to start putting baseballs on the batting tee in the batting cage.

Entering the ninth inning, with the score still 4–3, Athletics manager Tony LaRussa pulled starting pitcher Dave Stewart in favor of relief pitcher Dennis Eckersley. When the Dodgers saw Eckersley walk toward the mound, their hearts dropped.

Dennis Eckersley was the best relief pitcher in baseball that year. Hitters were baffled by his quirky sidearm delivery. His pitches seemed to appear at the plate out of nowhere. Eckersley had marvelous control and rarely walked a batter. When Eckersley entered a ball game, it was as good as over.

A few Dodgers players started to gather their hats and gloves. Maybe everyone was right, they thought. Maybe we were just lucky. Maybe we don't have enough to beat the A's, especially without Kirk.

Then, from underneath the stands, they heard something.

Thwack! Then a few seconds later, *Thwack!*

Gibson was hitting off the tee! He was going to try to play.

After taking only a few swings, Gibson turned to the batboy and said, "Tell Tommy if someone gets on, I want to hit." Poole ran to the dugout and gave Lasorda Gibson's message.

I think, Gibson added to himself, I've got one good swing left.

Dodgers catcher Mike Scioscia led off the ninth inning. He popped out. The Dodger players just sat on the bench, staring at the ground and crossing their fingers.

Then third baseman Jeff Hamilton stepped to the plate. A few pitches later, he returned to the dugout, dragging his bat behind him. Eckersley had struck him out.

Tommy Lasorda called shortstop Alfredo Griffin back from the on-deck circle and sent outfielder Mike Davis to the plate to pinch-hit. Davis, a former member of the A's, had a powerful swing. Lasorda was hoping for a home run to tie the game. In extra innings, anything could happen.

Davis refused to give in to the relief pitcher. After each pitch, he stepped out of the batter's box and calmly took a few practice swings.

The strategy unnerved Eckersley. He had walked only nine hitters unintentionally all year, but all of a sudden he couldn't find the plate.

Gibson kept swinging as he listened to the game on television. Davis worked the count to three balls and one strike.

Gibson stopped swinging. Eckersley wound up and threw another pitch.

Gibson heard the crowd roar. Ball four! Davis was on base.

Gibson turned to the batboy. "Mitch," he said, "this could be our script." Then he started walking toward the dugout.

Dodgers manager Tommy Lasorda pulled pinch hitter Dave Anderson back from the on-deck circle. Everyone in Dodger Stadium stared toward the Dodgers bench.

The home plate umpire walked over to the dugout. "Tommy," he called to the Dodgers manager, "you've got to have a hitter."

Lasorda looked up at the umpire. "I've got a hitter," he announced.

Just then, Gibson emerged from the runway into the Dodgers' dugout. As he gingerly climbed the steps leading from the dugout to the field, the fans caught sight of him. Everyone stood and cheered.

Gibson grabbed a bat and slowly limped onto the field. Underneath his uniform, everyone could see the bandages wrapped around his left thigh and right knee. His knees barely bent as he walked stiffly to the plate, like a mummy.

The fans stayed on their feet, cheering and hoping.

Gibson carefully dug in, trying to ignore the pain that shot through his legs each time he moved. Dennis Eckersley leaned over, took the sign from his catcher, and threw.

Gibson flailed at the pitch, fouled it back, and nearly fell over. He stepped out of the batter's box and bent over, sucking air between his teeth and waiting for the sharp pain shooting from his right knee to fade.

The cheers from the crowd abruptly faded. Strike one.

Gibson dug in once again. Once again, Eckersley hurled a pitch to the plate.

Gibson swung. As he stepped into the pitch, his legs nearly gave out from under him. He waved weakly at the ball and fouled it back again. Strike two.

Gibson stepped from the batter's box once more and tried to collect himself. One swing, he said to himself. I've got one good swing left. Then he stepped back in, cocked the bat behind his ear, and waited.

Eckersley was ahead, 0 and 2. He thought Gibson might be anxious. He threw his next pitch a fraction of an inch outside.

Gibson barely topped the ball. It slowly spun down the line, inches foul. The count was still 0 and 2.

Eckersley threw again. Gibson turned and watched the ball rocket into the catcher's mitt. Then he looked at the umpire.

Ball. The crowd started cheering again. The count was 1 and 2.

Eckersley was still ahead. He threw another pitch to the same place.

Gibson didn't move, but on first base, Mike Davis broke for second base. The Oakland catcher caught the ball and threw toward second.

"Safe!" yelled the second base umpire. And the home plate ump said, "Ball two."

Everyone in the stands jumped up and leaned toward the field, trying to get as close as possible. This was the situation everyone who has ever played or watched baseball has dreamed about: the World Series, the ninth inning, two outs, one run behind, one man on. Everyone was dreaming the same dream.

Gibson was still thinking about the one good swing

he had promised himself. He knew he couldn't step into the pitch the way he usually did. If Eckersley threw to the outside corner, he wouldn't be able to reach it. His legs were useless.

But there was nothing wrong with his arms. All he needed was an inside pitch, one he could pull with his arms and wrists and by turning his body.

Eckersley took a moment to size Gibson up. Even though Gibson was obviously in pain, Eckersley was a veteran. He knew that if he threw the wrong pitch, Gibson might be able to hit it.

He decided to throw a slider. He suspected Gibson would be looking for a pitch outside, since with his injuries, he wouldn't be able to step away from the plate and pull the ball. An inside pitch should jam him, thought Eckersley. He decided to throw the ball inside.

The Dodger players crowded to the top of the dugout steps.

Gibson dug in one last time. One good swing, he was thinking, I've got to have just one good swing.

Eckersley toed the rubber and took the sign from his catcher.

Eckersley wound up. He threw.

The ball sailed toward the plate, inside, but not too far inside. Low, but not too low.

Gibson stood with the bat waving in the air over his shoulder. He saw the pitch come in. He saw the pitch dip down.

He took a tiny step and shifted his weight to his front foot. He dropped his bat down, then swung with all his strength, twisting his upper body to make up for the weakness in his legs.

One good swing left.

Crack! The fat part of the bat met the ball just before it reached the plate.

The ball jumped from the bat and sailed in the air to right field.

As Gibson followed through, his momentum carried him away from the plate. He took a short, awkward step and tried to stay upright.

Dennis Eckersley spun around and watched the ball fly toward right field.

Tommy Lasorda stepped out of the dugout with his hands in the air and looked for the ball against the sky.

Outfielder Jose Canseco started backpedaling toward the right field wall.

Then he slowed. Stopped. Turned around.

Gibson regained his balance and stood at the plate, watching, as the ball dropped from the sky . . .

. . . and landed over the fence! Home run!

Tommy Lasorda jumped into the air and raised his arms toward the sky. Dodgers fans started leaping up and down and hugging each other. Dennis Eckersley stood absolutely still, then turned and started to walk off the field.

The game was over. The Dodgers had won, 5–4!

Gibson started around the bases, pumping his fist in the air. But he couldn't run; his legs hurt too bad to do that. They barely left the ground as he shuffled toward first, hardly strong enough to carry him down the line.

The fans continued to cheer as Gibson made a slow tour of the bases, Davis racing for home ahead of him. The entire Dodgers team gathered around home plate, waiting.

Tommy Lasorda was so happy, he started hugging everyone. Then he started pulling his players away from the baseline, making sure Gibson would have a clear path home.

Gibson gingerly rounded third and saw his teammates waiting for him. He slowly jogged toward them, spotted home plate in their midst, then hopped into the air and landed on it with both feet before disappearing into a mob of Dodgers uniforms.

The Dodgers went on to beat the A's in four of five games to win the World Series. Gibson, his legs still sore, didn't play another minute in the Series.

His one good swing had been just enough.

JIM ABBOTT
Just One Out Away

Nobody expected anything particularly special from Jim Abbott when he took the mound for the New York Yankees on September 4, 1993. Every game Jim Abbott pitched in the big leagues was already something special. In his short career, what was most special about Abbott had already become ordinary.

When Jim was growing up in Flint, Michigan, strangers would see him playing and frown. "That poor boy," they'd say, "what's wrong with his arm?"

Jim was born with only one full arm. His right arm is several inches shorter than his left. And on the end of his right arm is just one tiny finger.

But that never prevented Jim from doing what everyone else did. His parents never let him use his arm as an excuse to back away from a challenge.

People didn't pity Jim Abbott for long. Even with only one good arm, Jim was one of the best athletes in his neighborhood. He could dribble a basketball, pass, and shoot with his left arm. He could throw a football farther than most other boys. But Jim loved playing baseball the best.

At first, baseball was hard for Jim to play. He had to figure out how to field the ball with his left hand, get the glove off his hand, get the ball out of his glove, then throw the ball — and he had to do it as quickly as players who could field with one hand and throw with the other.

Every day, when Jim's dad came home from work, they played catch. When his dad wasn't home, Jim took his ball and glove and threw against a brick wall, pretending he was Nolan Ryan. After each pitch, Jim had to figure out how to catch the ball. Each time he did, he became a little bit better.

With time and a lot of practice, Jim learned to balance his glove on the end of his right arm as he wound up and threw. As soon as he let the ball go, he slid his left hand into his glove. Then he fielded the ball, stuck his glove into the crook of his right arm, pulled his hand out, grabbed the ball, and threw it again.

After hours of practice, it was hard to see how Jim did it. The complicated move became automatic. And as he grew older, he kept getting better.

When Jim graduated from high school, he went to the University of Michigan on a baseball scholarship. He became one of the best pitchers in college baseball. In 1989 the California Angels made him their first pick in the baseball draft.

Some people didn't think Jim Abbott could play at the major league level. But the Angels believed in him. After all, he didn't let his right arm keep him from being one of the most promising rookies of the season, so why should *they*? The Angels didn't even send him to the minor leagues. He went from college straight to the majors.

Abbott played with the Angels for three years, then was traded to the Yankees after the 1992 season. They thought he was one of the best pitchers in baseball.

But for most of the 1993 season, Abbott didn't pitch very well. When other pitchers struggled, most people thought they were just going through a slump. When Abbott struggled, people started to think it might be because he had only one hand.

Abbott was unable to hide his pitching hand in his glove as other pitchers could. That made it hard for him to disguise his next pitch. Although he had been successful for several big league seasons, now some baseball people were blaming his hand for his problems on the mound.

Late in August of 1993, while pitching against the Indians in Cleveland, Abbott had the worst performance of his major league career. In less than four full innings, Abbott gave up ten hits and seven runs.

When Abbott returned to the clubhouse after being replaced, he yanked off his uniform, pulled on a pair of shorts and running shoes, then ran out of the clubhouse and onto the sidewalk around the stadium.

He wasn't trying to run away. He just ran, trying to shake the miserable feeling he had.

As he ran through the streets near the stadium, he wondered what was wrong with him. One thought raced through his head. Am I really good enough to pitch in the big leagues?

Abbott had always believed he could play major league baseball, even when no one else did. So far, he had proven that he was right.

But now he wondered. Maybe everyone else *was* right. He knew what they were starting to think. Maybe a one-armed man couldn't pitch in the big leagues.

Then Abbott realized what he was thinking. He started running just a little harder, pumping his left arm for balance, until he was almost sprinting. He *was* a major league pitcher. He had worked long and hard to reach the major leagues, and he wasn't about to quit now. He never had. He knew he could do better.

He turned around and headed back toward the stadium. Next time, he thought, I'll do better.

Abbott took the mound for his next start in Yankee Stadium a week later. It was a critical game for the Yankees. They were fighting for the division lead. Abbott knew the game was important for his team.

The Indians were a good hitting team. Their lineup included players like speedy Kenny Lofton, All-Star Carlos Baerga, and powerful Albert Belle. As he took the mound, Abbott remembered how poorly he had pitched against Cleveland a week before. He knew he would have to do better.

But five pitches later, Cleveland's first hitter, Kenny Lofton, walked.

Abbott tried not to think about the runner on first. He concentrated on the next hitter, Felix Fermin.

Abbott threw another pitch. Ball one.

He knew he couldn't afford to walk another hitter. He told himself to keep the ball down in the strike zone. He knew a batter was likely to hit a ground ball on a low pitch.

Abbott threw Fermin a low fastball. It went exactly where he wanted it to go. And sure enough, Fermin hit the ball on the ground. Kenny Lofton took off for second as Fermin dropped his bat and headed for first.

Yankee second baseman Mike Gallego fielded the ball and flipped it to shortstop Randy Velarde. Velarde stepped on second, then gunned the ball to first.

Double play! When the next hitter popped out, Abbott jogged off the mound. So far, so good. His confidence was coming back.

Abbott pitched even better in the second inning. His fastball sailed in on the batters, and his slider broke just where he wanted it to. He quickly struck out Cleveland's first batter, powerful Albert Belle.

Then he tried to pitch too carefully. He walked Randy Milligan.

Abbott took a deep breath and tried to concentrate. It worked. Indian outfielder Manny Ramirez flew out to Yankee center fielder Bernie Williams. Then Candy Maldonado struck out.

When Abbott returned to the Yankee bench, only catcher Matt Nokes came over to speak with him. Nokes told him to keep the ball down and relax.

Abbott retired the Indians in order in the third inning: three men up, three men out. Then, on their turn at bat, the Yankees exploded with three runs. When Abbott took the mound in the fourth, the score read New York 3, Cleveland 0.

When Abbott left the mound, the score hadn't changed. He had set the Indians down in order again.

The Yankes couldn't add to their lead in their turn at bat, and Abbott knew the Indians would be looking to catch up to them. For a moment, he lost his concentration. He walked leadoff batter Randy Milligan.

Abbott looked in at Indians hitter Manny Ramirez. He knew what to do next.

Abbott pitched carefully and threw a slider at Ramirez's knees. Ramirez hit a ground ball.

The Yankee infield came through again. Double play!

Then Candy Maldonado popped up for the third out. Abbott knew his pitching had helped keep the Indians from scoring. Yet when he returned to the bench, not even Matt Nokes came over to talk to him.

Everyone on the Yankee bench now knew that

Abbott could be throwing a no-hitter. Everyone in baseball believes it is bad luck to talk to a pitcher when he is throwing a no-hitter. No one wanted to jinx Jim Abbott.

It must have helped. The Yankees added another run to their lead in the bottom of the fifth inning, and in the sixth, the Indians were defenseless against Abbott's pitching. At the start of the seventh inning, the score read Yankees 4, Indians 0.

By now the crowd at Yankee Stadium had started to take note of Abbott's performance. When Abbott walked out to the mound to start the seventh inning, everyone stood and cheered. Abbott was tired, but the encouragement from the crowd gave him a boost. With three innings to go, he just tried to keep concentrating and throw strikes.

Carlos Baerga led off with a ground ball to first baseman Don Mattingly. Mattingly snuffed out the grounder and raced to touch the bag. One out.

Then Albert Belle, the Indians' most powerful hitter, stepped up to the plate.

Yankee third baseman Wade Boggs looked closely at the right-handed hitter. He knew Belle was a pull hitter, liable to hit the ball to left, so he took a small step closer to the line.

Sure enough, Belle swung and hit a vicious line drive down the third base line. Boggs instinctively dove to his left.

He stretched out as far as he could and stuck out his glove. Belle's line drive hit the ground, bounced — and stuck in Bogg's mitt.

As Belle charged toward first base, Boggs scrambled to his feet and came up throwing. Out! The crowd roared. They knew every pitcher throwing a no-hitter needed a few great plays behind him. Boggs had provided just that.

Abbott turned, looked at the third baseman, and gave him a little wave of his glove. Boggs understood. Abbott was saying thanks.

Abbott had had trouble with the next hitter, Randy Milligan, earlier in the game. But this time Milligan hit a routine ground ball to Boggs. Boggs threw him out at first. The crowd roared as Abbott jogged off the field.

The Yankees didn't add to their lead in their next turn at bat. But by now, all anyone wanted to see was what Jim Abbott would do on the mound. Abbott didn't disappoint.

Energized by the cheers of the crowd, he struck out Manny Ramirez to lead off the eighth. Candy

Maldonado then grounded out, but Abbott walked Jim Thome.

Indians catcher Sandy Alomar stepped in. He hit another easy ground ball, to third base. Boggs flipped it to second for the forced out.

Jim Abbott was now three outs away from a no-hitter.

Abbott had never pitched a no-hitter in the major leagues. Just thinking about a no-hitter made him nervous. He tried to stay calm as he took the mound in the ninth inning.

Kenny Lofton led off. Abbott hoped he would hit the ball hard, but right at someone. Lofton was one of the fastest players in the league, and Abbott didn't want to lose a no-hitter on an infield hit.

On the first pitch, Lofton squared around to bunt. The ball hit his bat and rolled foul.

The crowd started to boo. They thought Lofton was trying to take advantage of Abbott.

Abbott didn't think so. He knew that Lofton bunted on every pitcher in the league, and he wasn't treating Abbott any differently. Lofton was just trying to get on base and help his team win.

Lofton swung at the next pitch, and the ball bounced toward second — slowly. Yankee infielder

Mike Gallego charged in, fielded the ball, and flipped it to first in one continuous motion.

Don Mattingly stretched toward the throw as Lofton rocketed toward first.

The umpire's hand shot up in the air. "Out!"

Jim Abbott was now two outs away from pitching a no-hitter.

The crowd stood as Abbott looked in and took the sign from Matt Nokes. Light-hitting shortstop Felix Fermin stepped to the plate.

Abbott threw. The ball sailed right down the middle of the plate.

Fermin swung. He hit the ball as hard as he could toward center field.

Yankee center fielder Bernie Williams was playing Fermin shallow. He heard the crack of the bat on the ball, turned, and ran toward the center field fence.

The ball drifted back. Williams ran hard. Just as he reached the warning track, he stuck out his glove — and caught the ball.

Out! Jim Abbott was one out away.

Carlos Baerga stepped to the plate and dug in.

Abbott looked at him curiously. Baerga was a switch-hitter. Normally he batted from the right side against the left-handed pitcher.

This time Baerga stepped in on the left side. In his previous at bats, Abbott had jammed him with his fastball. Baerga thought that if he batted from the left side, he'd have a better chance to hit the ball.

Abbott looked in. He didn't care what side Baerga hit from. He was going to pitch the only way he knew how.

He wound up and threw. As he let the ball go, he tucked his hand into his glove and pulled it off his right arm, ready to field the ball.

Baerga swung late. The ball bounded to the left side of the infield. Abbott lunged toward the ball, but it bounced past him.

He turned and saw shortstop Randy Velarde racing in. Baerga, having swung from the left side, had a head start toward first.

Velarde charged in, his glove low to the ground. He scooped up Baerga's ball on the short hop, then threw to first without breaking stride.

Mattingly stretched for the throw as Baerga neared the base. He caught it as Baerga streaked across the bag.

For a second no one moved. The play was close.

"Out!" The umpire's hand shot into the air. The

crowd went wild. Jim Abbott had just pitched a no-hitter!

On the mound, Abbott raised his arms in triumph and smiled as his Yankees teammates surrounded him. Abbott gave his teammates high fives with his left hand.

As the fans stood and applauded, they weren't just applauding Jim Abbott, the one-armed pitcher. They were applauding Jim Abbott, the major leaguer who had just done something special.

THE BOSTON RED SOX
Reversing the Curse

"Hey, little man."

A young boy rolled over and looked at his clock. It was nearly midnight. Then he looked at his mother. She was leaning over his bed, smiling. Even though the room was dark, he could make out the baseball cap she was wearing. It was navy blue and had a red *B* on it. There was an identical cap on his bed stand beside him.

Suddenly he realized why his mother was waking him up. He sat bolt upright.

"Is it over?" he asked, his voice full of hope. "Did the Red Sox win the World Series?"

She smiled. "Not yet. There's one inning left in the game. Your dad and grandfather are watching it downstairs. Come on. Let's watch with them."

"Really?" The boy couldn't believe it. His mother had never let him stay up so late before!

94

"Really," she assured him. "After all, we could be witnessing history!"

The boy slipped out of bed. As he followed her out of his room, he let his eyes travel over the posters he'd put on his walls. For the last several months, Curt Schilling, Johnny Damon, David Ortiz, Kevin Millar, Jason Varitek, and the rest of the Boston Red Sox team had greeted him every time he'd come into his bedroom. But even without the posters he'd have known who they were. After all, he'd spent the past spring, summer, and early fall following their every game; charting their stats with his friends; and hoping, sometimes even praying, that come the end of October, they'd be world champs.

And now here they were: one inning away from realizing that dream.

It had been a long time coming — eighty-six years, in fact! The last time the Boston Red Sox had won the World Series was in 1918. Before that they'd taken the championship four times — in 1903, 1912, 1915, and 1916. But even though they'd come close to winning since 1918 — they'd been to the Series four more times, in 1946, 1967, 1975, and 1986 — they'd never won.

This year, the Red Sox had ended the regular

2004 season with the club's highest number of wins, 98, since 1975. They had trounced the Anaheim Angels in the division playoffs, winning three games in a row. Then, in the American League Championship, they had made history.

In that best-out-of-seven series, the Sox had faced their longtime archrivals, the New York Yankees. These two teams had met in the AL Championships twice before, once in 1999 and once in 2003. Both times, New York had emerged victorious.

After three games, all of which New York won, it appeared that the Yankees were going to eliminate the Sox yet again. New York needed just one more win to cut the Sox out of the World Series. Boston, on the other hand, had to win four games in a row to advance to the Series.

Statistically, that seemed impossible. No team in the history of Major League Baseball had *ever* come from behind like that to win the AL Championships.

Yet the Red Sox didn't give up. In the bottom of the ninth of the fourth game, the score was 4–3, Yankees. The Sox were three outs away from elimination. Then the Yankees pitcher, Mariano Rivera, walked the first batter, Kevin Millar. Pinch runner Dave Roberts took Millar's place on first, but he didn't stay there long.

Instead, he stole second. He didn't stay there long, either, for on the next pitch Bill Mueller hit a single — and Roberts crossed home plate to tie it up, 4–4.

The score was still tied at the bottom of the twelfth. Then Boston's star left fielder, Manny Ramirez, laid down a single. Next up was David Ortiz, the Red Sox designated hitter. And hit he did — a home run to right field! The Sox won the game, 6–4. The AL Championships weren't over yet.

The next night, Ortiz was the hero again. This time his game-winning smash home run came in the fourteenth inning! Now at three games to two, the Series was a whole lot closer. And when they won the game the following night, it was suddenly anybody's ball game.

The last game of the series was played in New York before a sold-out crowd. Both teams were exhausted from the two previous overtime games, but the Sox had something the Yankees seemed to lack: momentum. They rocketed on to a 10–3 win in nine innings — and made history by becoming the first team ever to change a three-game deficit to a four-game victory.

And now, with three wins under their belt and the score of the fourth game at 3–0, Boston, the Sox were on the verge of making history again, this time by winning their first championship in eighty-six years.

The young boy padded into the living room and climbed onto the couch between his father and grandfather. The bottom of the ninth inning was about to start.

"Sure wish my dad was still alive to watch this with me," his grandfather whispered to him. "He would have liked to see his team win the Series again."

"Your dad used to follow the Sox, too?" the boy asked incredulously.

"He did indeed," the old man replied with a smile. "In fact, he saw them win the Series in 1918! He was just a little guy like you then. He always believed they'd win another one."

"Just like me," the boy said. He pointed to the T-shirt he was wearing. *I believe in the Red Sox Nation!* it proclaimed in bold letters.

The second half of the inning began. Pitcher Kevin Foulke was on the mound for the Sox. He reared back and hurled the ball toward the first St. Louis batter, Albert Pujols.

Strike!

Foulke got the ball back from catcher Jason Variteck. Threw again. This time, the pitch was called for a ball. On the third pitch, Pujols got a piece of the ball but knocked it foul. Two strikes. Pujols fouled the next pitch, too, but on the fifth he cracked the ball into center field for a single.

Man on first. No outs.

"Come on, come on, come on," the boy whispered. "Get 'em out of there!"

Scott Rolen stepped up to the plate. Foulke took the signal from Varitek and threw.

Strike one!

Foulke threw again. Rolen swung. Missed.

Strike two!

Foulke's next pitch was called for a ball. Then Rolen sent the ball rocketing into right field. Trot Nixon stuck out a glove and caught it.

One out.

Jim Edmonds strode to the batter's box. Three swings later, he left.

Two outs.

The boy clutched his father's and grandfather's hands and squeezed tightly.

Edgar Renteria came to the plate. Foulke threw. Renteria watched it go by for a ball.

Suddenly, Pujols took off from first. He dove into the dirt at second.

There was one out yet to go and a St. Louis player in scoring position.

The boy sucked in his breath and held it.

Foulke twirled the ball in his hand. He got the signal from Varitek and reared back and threw.

Renteria connected — and sent the ball bouncing back toward Foulke.

"Get it! Get it!" the boy, his parents, and grandfather screamed as Renteria took off down the line. Foulke fielded the ball. He jogged a few steps toward first baseman Doug Mientkiewicz. Then, with a move that seemed almost casual, he tossed the ball.

Mientkiewicz caught it. Stepped on the bag.

Three outs. Game over! *The Red Sox had won the World Series!*

The boy jumped up and down, yelling and cheering at the top of his lungs. His parents hugged and laughed. At the ballpark, the Red Sox players launched themselves into one another's arms. Fans poured onto the field to celebrate with their home team, the new world champs.

The boy's grandfather swept him into his arms and twirled him around the room.

"I believed, Grandpa," the boy whispered. "Just like your dad did."

The old man smiled. "I'll bet wherever he is, he's celebrating, too."

Matt Christopher®

Sports Bio Bookshelf

Muhammad Ali

Lance Armstrong

Kobe Bryant

Jennifer Capriati

Dale Earnhardt, Sr.

Jeff Gordon

Ken Griffey Jr.

Mia Hamm

Tony Hawk

Ichiro

Derek Jeter

Randy Johnson

Michael Jordan

Mario Lemieux

Mark McGwire

Yao Ming

Shaquille O'Neal

Jackie Robinson

Alex Rodriguez

Babe Ruth

Curt Schilling

Sammy Sosa

Venus and Serena Williams

Tiger Woods

Read them all!

Baseball Flyhawk

Baseball Pals

Baseball Turnaround

The Basket Counts

Body Check

Catch That Pass!

Catcher with a Glass Arm

Catching Waves

Center Court Sting

Centerfield Ballhawk

Challenge at Second Base

The Comeback Challenge

Comeback of the Home Run Kid

Cool as Ice

The Diamond Champs

Dirt Bike Racer

Dirt Bike Runaway

Dive Right In

Double Play at Short

Face-Off

Fairway Phenom

Football Fugitive

Football Nightmare

The Fox Steals Home

Goalkeeper in Charge

The Great Quarterback Switch

Halfback Attack*

The Hockey Machine

Ice Magic

Inline Skater

Johnny Long Legs

The Kid Who Only Hit Homers

*Previously published as Crackerjack Halfback

All available in paperback from Little, Brown and Company

**Previously published as Pressure Play